FOR THE LOVE OF BAKING!

This ~~cake~~ book belongs to...

_____

Copyright © 2023 Elyse Hadeed

For the Love of Baking! is a fun book created by Elyse Hadeed of EH Creations Co. All rights reserved. No part of this book covered by the copyright herein may be reproduced, stored in a retrieval system, or transmitted in any form or by any means, without the prior permission in writing of the copyright owner.

ISBN: 978-1-7380723-0-9

Author: Elyse Hadeed
Illustrator: Rachael Mc Farlane-Francique

EH Creations Co.
Stoney Creek, Ontario, Canada
Social Media: @ehcreationsco

This book is dedicated to my little one, Oliver, and my loving husband Marc. Thank you for inspiring and supporting me to do what I love!

This Edition: 2023
Printed in the United States of America.

A birthday cake does not come just so!

There is so much more to baking
than you may know.

Let's go to the kitchen where we will start by choosing a recipe,
whether it be sweet or tart.

This time we can make a cake,
and next time a pie,
you won't know which is your favourite
unless you try.

Baking is a process
in which steps cannot be skipped,
or else our baked goods
will have something amiss.

Most importantly to start,
we must wash our hands,
before we prepare the baking pans.

We must read instructions carefully

FAVOURITE RECIPE

1.
2.
3.
4.

← Recipe

and gather our tools and ingredients,

↳ Butter

Measuring Cup

an important step, I must say, because I have learned from experience.

Spatula

Oil

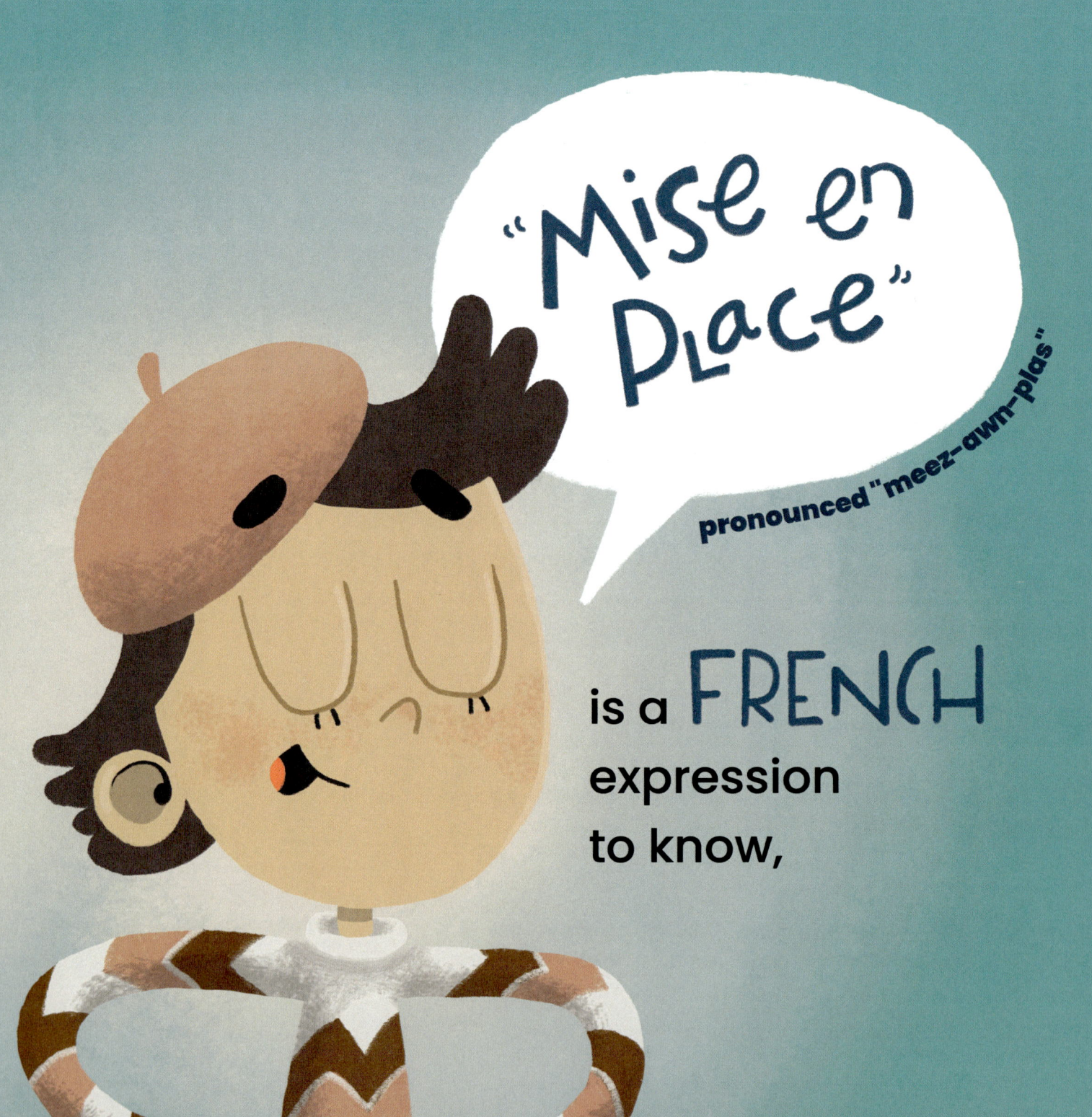

which means
"everything must be in its place"
before we can go!

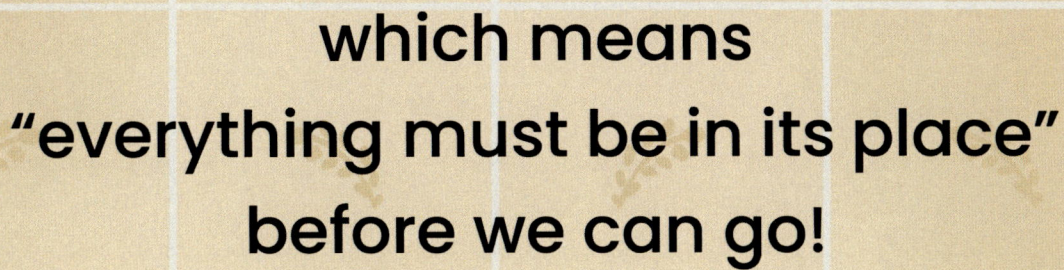

Don't forget the

as they add up to make one *big* cake for you.

The world of baking is so much **MORE** than food!

Math,

¼ cup of butter

reading,

Fold in the flour

problem solving, and science
are also included too!

Fractions and weights, add up to create a cake.

But cannot work alone without chemistry taking place.

Changing from a liquid to a solid state or from one colour to another, occurs when our ingredients are interacting with each other.

And don't forget the heat

that pulls it all together,

as we wait patiently to see what we uncover.

Creativity is guaranteed to follow, as you prepare to decorate using **COLOURS**, *icing,* and even **MARSHMALLOWS**!

And remember to check the substitution list.

Take a chance at making a favourite with a fun little twist!

And one last thing
that is important to note!
The bonds you create
will be your favourite thing
that baking promotes.

So, roll your sleeves up
and put on your apron,
because kid,
you are going to love baking!

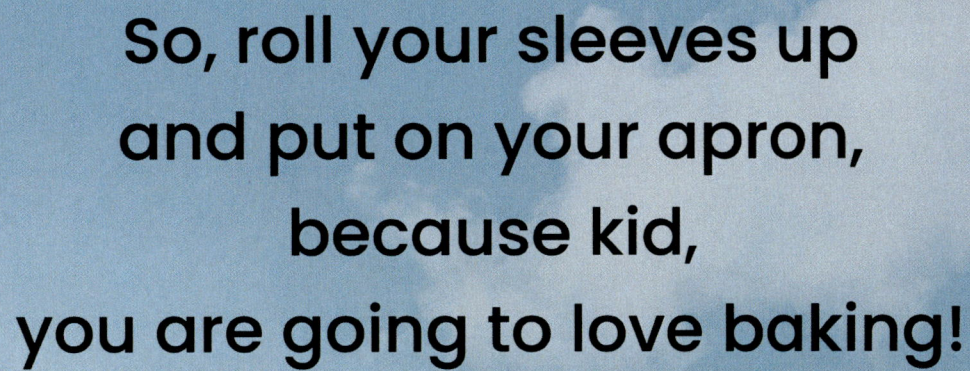

Scrumptious Chocolate Cake

Prep Time: 25 mins | Cook Time: 30-35 mins | Total time: 1 hour

Makes two 9-inch round cake layers

TOOLS:

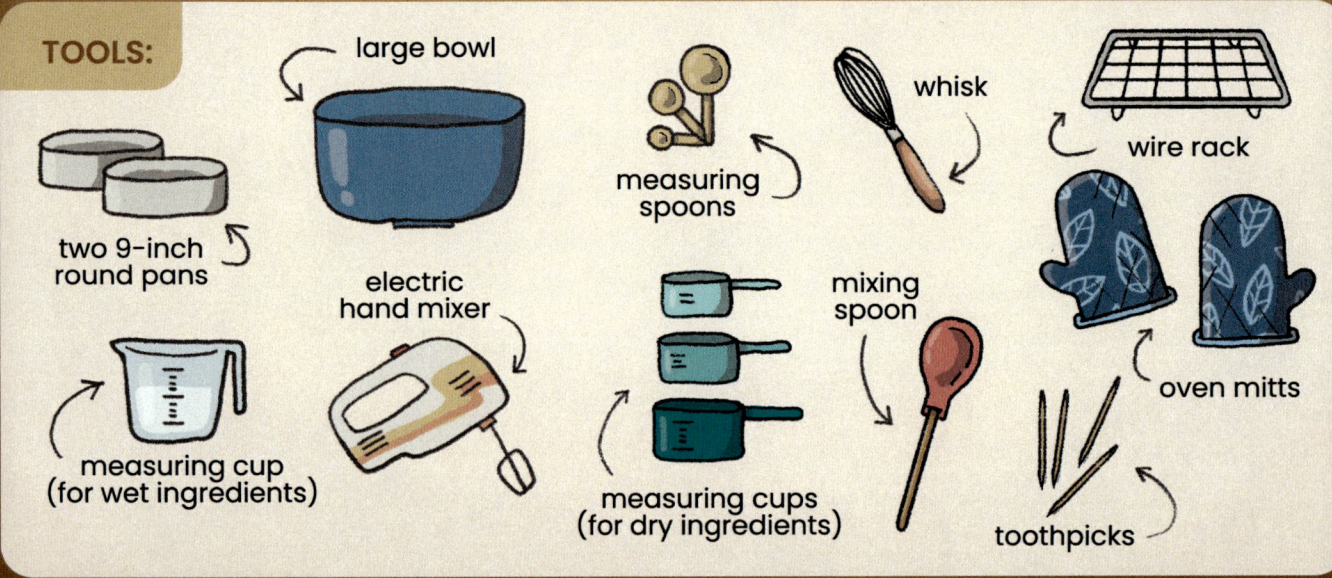

- two 9-inch round pans
- large bowl
- measuring spoons
- whisk
- wire rack
- electric hand mixer
- measuring cups (for dry ingredients)
- mixing spoon
- oven mitts
- measuring cup (for wet ingredients)
- toothpicks

INGREDIENTS:

- 2 cups white sugar
- 1¾ cups all-purpose flour
- ¾ cups unsweetened cocoa powder
- 1½ tsp. baking powder
- 1½ tsp. baking soda
- 1 tsp. salt
- 2 large eggs
- 1 cup milk
- ½ cup vegetable oil
- 2 tsp. vanilla extract (pure or imitation)
- 1 cup boiling water
- non-stick vegetable spray

Footnote: tsp. = teaspoon, tbsp. = tablespoon

STEP 1

Gather your tools and ingredients and lay them out.

pronounced "meez-awn-plas" "Mise en Place"

STEP 2

Turn the oven on and set to 350°F.

STEP 3

Grease the cake pans.

Set them aside.

STEP 4

In the large bowl, add the...

- 2 cups of sugar
- 1¾ cups of flour
- ¾ cup of cocoa powder
- 1½ tsp. of baking powder
- 1½ tsp. of baking soda
- 1 tsp. of salt

STEP 5

Stir with the whisk  to mix ingredients together and ensure there are no clumps.

STEP 6

Next, add in...

Mix with  on medium speed for **2 minutes**.

STEP 7

Add in the  of hot water.

Using the spoon stir the batter well. The batter will be thin; this is normal.

STEP 8

Pour the batter evenly into the cake pans.

Put in the oven and bake for  30 to 35 minutes.

STEP 9

To ensure the cake is fully baked, insert a toothpick / into the centre.

If it comes out clean, it's ready!

STEP 10

If there is still batter on it, put it back in the oven for a few more minutes, then re-test!

STEP 11

Once baked, using your oven mitts , take them out of the oven and cool the pans for ⏲ minutes.

STEP 12

Then, remove the cakes from the pan and finish cooling on a wire rack 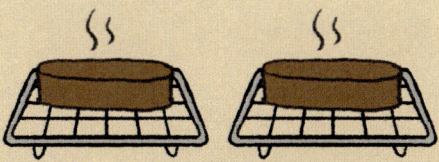.

Once fully cooled, you are ready to decorate!

NOTES:

If you don't have non-stick spray to grease the pans, use butter and flour. Use your clean hand or a paper towel and spread the butter around the pan and the sides too! Then, lightly sprinkle with flour overtop the butter.

Use your favourite ready-made icing to ice your cake or try the homemade buttercream icing provided.

For egg-free, use 2/3 cups of unsweetened applesauce in place of the eggs. Just note, the cake may need to bake a few extra minutes.

For a fun twist, add different toppings such as nuts, fruits, sprinkles , even more chocolate, marshmallows, etc. You can even try a cream cheese icing! The sky's the limit, enjoy experimenting!

most importantly, Have fun and make memories!!

Chocolate Buttercream Icing

Prep Time: 20 mins | Total time: 20 mins

Makes 3 cups

TOOLS: small bowl, medium bowl, large bowl, measuring spoons, whisk, measuring cups (for dry ingredients), electric hand mixer, spatula

INGREDIENTS: 1 cup unsalted butter, softened; ¾ cups cocoa powder; 1 tsp. vanilla extract (pure or imitation); 4 cups powdered (icing) sugar; 3-4 tbsp. milk

STEP 1

In the medium bowl, add...

4 cups of powdered (icing) sugar

Stir with the whisk so there are no clumps. Set aside.

STEP 2

In the small bowl, add...

¾ cups of cocoa powder

Stir with the whisk so there are no clumps. Set aside.

STEP 3

In the large bowl, add... 1 cup of unsalted butter, softened

and mix with a mixer until fluffy and pale yellow. Approximately **3 minutes**.

STEP 4

Next, add in the cocoa powder and... 1 tsp. of vanilla extract

Mix well with the mixer .

STEP 5

Mix the powdered sugar in, 1 cup at a time. Beat on medium speed. Use the spatula to scrape down the sides and bottom of the bowl often.

STEP 6

The icing will be dry, so add in 3-4 tbsp. of milk and beat on medium speed until light and fluffy.

Transfer cooled cake to a plate and you are now ready to decorate!

For the Love of Baking

```
S  Q  T  A  C  A  K  E  M  K
S  F  A  P  R  O  N  M  J  V
H  A  F  Q  S  N  L  Z  B  J
S  M  O  K  U  M  L  R  A  Y
E  I  V  F  H  N  M  I  K  R
K  L  E  I  C  I  N  G  I  E
C  Y  N  N  Y  T  O  J  N  C
D  U  M  F  N  O  R  A  G  I
S  P  R  I  N  K  L  E  S  P
X  G  M  I  X  I  N  G  G  E
```

APRON
CAKE
FUN
MIXING
RECIPE

BAKING
FAMILY
ICING
OVEN
SPRINKLES

For the Love of Baking

APRON
CAKE
FUN
MIXING
RECIPE

BAKING
FAMILY
ICING
OVEN
SPRINKLES

Manufactured by Amazon.ca
Bolton, ON